Creating a Financial Plan

The Blueprint for Wealth Acquisition

Table of Contents

Chapter 1. Introduction

In today's fluctuating economic climate, fortifying your financial future has never been more paramount. "Creating a Financial Plan: The Blueprint for Wealth Acquisition" is a meticulously crafted Special Report that acknowledges this necessity, promising to dispel the intricate curtains of financial planning. We effortlessly distill this seemingly complex subject down to its bare essentials, providing an accessible roadmap toward wealth acquisition tailored explicitly for your life goals. This report, written in easy-to-understand language, doesn't just outline how to manage your finances; it equips you with tangible skills and knowledge to foster a vibrant financial health radiating with potential growth. If you've been seeking out a comprehensive guide, a beacon in the storm of financial strategy, then consider this Special Report as your long-awaited catalyst for change towards a more secure, prosperous future. Get ready to turn the page towards your financial freedom!

Chapter 2. Understanding Financial Planning: The Basics

Before delving into the realm of financial planning, it's crucial to familiarize oneself with the most basic concepts. This knowledge acts as the bedrock from which more complex financial planning strategies stem. Understanding these concepts isn't just about managing money; it's about harnessing its potential to work in your favor.

2.1. Defining Financial Planning

Financial planning, at its core, is the process of constructing a roadmap to achieve financial goals. This involves setting clear, measurable goals, understanding your current financial status, creating a plan to reach the goals, and monitoring the progress on an ongoing basis. It is a process that integrates various aspects of a person's finances, encompassing budgeting, investment, insurance, and tax management.

Crucially, financial planning is not a one-time thing. It's an ongoing process that requires regular reviews and adjustments as your financial circumstances and personal goals evolve in time. Lifelong events like marriage, parenthood, education, retirement, and estate planning can trigger financial adjustments and drive a review of your plan.

2.2. Establishing Financial Goals

Financial planning begins with setting goals. A financial goal is a monetary amount that you aim to achieve in a predefined time frame. Goals can range from short term (a year or less), to medium term (1 to 5 years) and long term (more than 5 years).

Short-term goals might include saving for a vacation or paying off a small debt, while medium-term goals may consist of saving for a down payment on a house or achieving a certain net worth. On the other hand, long-term goals are often focused on retirement, children's education, or estate planning.

Every individual or family's goals are different, but they should all be Specific, Measurable, Achievable, Realistic, and Timely (SMART). This framework ensures that goals inspire action and are not left as vague aspirations.

2.3. Analyzing Your Financial Status

Once goals are in place, the next step is to analyze your current financial status. This involves documenting your income, expenses, assets, and liabilities.

Your income consists of all earnings, including salaries, part-time wages, dividend income, and any other sources.

Expenses, on the other hand, are everything you spend money on within a specific time period. This includes your living expenses, leisure activities, health expenses, insurance premiums, and so on.

After detailing your income and expenses, the leftover amount is what you have to save. If you spend more than you earn, you're running a deficit—a situation you'll need to rectify by either increasing your income or cutting back on expenses.

Your assets include cash, investments, property, and other items of value, while liabilities consist of any money you owe, like loans, personal dues, or credit card bills. The difference between your assets and liabilities represents your net worth, a key indicator of your financial health.

2.4. Creating Your Financial Plan

With a clear understanding of your financial status and goals, you can now create a financial plan. This involves distributing your savings and investments in a way that aligns with your goals. The type of allocation depends on various factors, such as the time frame of your goals, your risk tolerance, and your financial requirements.

For short-term goals, safety of capital is usually prioritized, so investments could go into safe, liquid investments like fixed deposits, money market funds, or short-term bonds.

Medium-term goals require a balance of safety and growth. You could invest in a mix of equity and bonds through low-cost index funds or balanced mutual funds.

For long-term goals, the key is growth. Investments are often directed to assets with high return potential like equities, real estate, or growth-focused mutual funds.

Along with investing, your financial plan should include insurance coverage and an emergency fund to deal with unexpected life events without derailing your financial plan.

2.5. Monitoring and Adjustments

Once your financial plan is in place, monitoring becomes significant. Always review your plan at least annually, and whenever there are significant changes in your life.

This is necessary as changes in income, expenses, or financial goals can impact your plan. Additionally, the performance of your investments can lead to potential rebalancing of your portfolio.

Adjustments might involve changing your investment mix, investing more or less, changing your insurance coverage, or resetting financial goals. Regular reviews and adjustments ensure that the financial plan evolves with your life, significantly increasing chances of achieving your goals.

In conclusion, financial planning is a dynamic process that begins with understanding and establishing your financial position and goals. It involves creating an actionable plan that includes saving, investing, and protecting your finances, and frequent reviews to keep the plan relevant and effective. By mastering the basics of financial planning, you put yourself on the road toward a secure, financially stable future.

Chapter 3. Structuring Your Financial Goals: Short-Term vs Long-Term

Stepping into financial planning can feel like diving into a deep abyss without a life jacket. The waters swirl, bringing in countless variables that seem impossible to predict. And yet, a robust financial plan is key to a thriving and secure future. As we embark on the journey of making sense of this intricate web of financial underpinnings, it's crucial to start by delineating our financial goals and structuring them accordingly. This layout becomes our compass, guiding our every step towards prosperity.

3.1. Defining Financial Goals

Every journey begins with a destination. In the realm of financial planning, the destination is your financial goals, the milestones you want to achieve. These goals could range from buying a house, retiring early to achieving financial independence, or saving for your child's education. To stitch together an effective plan, you first need to identify what these financial goals are.

Start by writing them down on paper. Make a list of all the short-term and long-term goals you want to achieve. It could help to categorize them further into needs, wants, and loves to prioritize them better. Once you have your list, chalk out a rough timeframe for each goal. This division allows you to create an actionable plan that is both time-bound and flexible.

3.2. Short-Term Financial Goals

Short-term financial goals are typically those you want to achieve within the next five years. They may range from paying off a credit card debt, saving for a vacation, or accumulating funds for down payment on a home.

The first step in achieving these goals is creating a budget. This exercise provides a clear view of your income, expenses, debts, and savings. It's the foundation for practical, realistic goal setting. Make sure you maintain an emergency fund as part of this budget to cover unexpected expenses.

Next, strategize how to maximize your savings for these goals. Consider low-risk investment options that can yield reasonable returns within your timeframe. Savings accounts, money market accounts, or short-term bonds are common vehicles for short-term financial goals.

Lastly, consistently track and reassess your progress towards these goals. Use tools and apps that can help you monitor your spending, saving, and investments. Be prepared to reassess and adjust goals based on changes in your financial situation.

3.3. Transitioning from Short-Term to Long-Term Goals

The journey from short-term financial goals to long-term ones can seem daunting, but it's a gradual and viable transition. It often involves balancing repayment of debts, growing savings, and embarking on suitable investments.

Ensure that you tackle high-interest debts first. Fast-tracking repayment of these debts not only relieves financial stress but frees up more of your income for savings and investments.

At this stage, it might be worth considering slightly riskier investments. Medium-term bonds, mutual funds, and direct equity are a few options that provide higher returns for slightly higher risk.

Assess your insurance plan needs at this transition stage, including life, health, and disability. The right insurance policies add a layer of protection, cushioning you from potential financial shocks.

3.4. Long-Term Financial Goals

Long-term financial goals are those you hope to reach in more than five years. They are often significant life events, including saving for your kids' university education, planning for retirement, or purchasing property.

In order to meet these goals, it's imperative to consider higher-growth, higher-risk investment vehicles such as stocks or real estate. The extended time frame allows you to ride out fluctuations in the market and stand a chance to earn substantial returns. It's essential, however, to research thoroughly and consult with a financial advisor before jumping into these options.

You should also focus on growing your wealth by reinvesting the returns you earn. This approach, called compounding, is a potent long-term wealth-building strategy.

Retirement planning should be a significant part of your long-term financial goals. Various options, such as employer-sponsored plans, Individual Retirement Accounts (IRAs), and self-managed super funds (SMSFs), can help build a robust retirement corpus.

3.5. Regular Review and Adjustments

Financial planning is not a "set-it-and-forget-it" exercise. Regular reviews and adjustments to your goals as per personal life milestones, market conditions, and financial performance are vital.

These reviews can prevent shortsighted decisions and retain your focus on the larger financial picture.

Remember, the journey of financial planning is personal and unique. While this text provides a roadmap, your journey's intricacies will vary. However, with patience, perseverance, and consistency, a solid financial future is within reach. Today's efforts will significantly enhance your tomorrow, leading you towards a more secure and prosperous future.

Chapter 4. The Art of Budgeting: Building Your Personal Economy

One of the cornerstone concepts of sound financial planning lies in mastering the art of budgeting. Budgeting, in essence, is about balancing your income against your expenses to ensure you live within your means, while also setting aside funds for future goals and unexpected emergencies.

4.1. Understanding your Cash Flow

Commence your budgeting journey by dissecting your cash flow. The first step is to itemize your income sources. Identify all your revenue streams, from your regular paycheck to any additional earnings like commissions, bonuses, interest or dividends from investments, side income, etc. This will help you ascertain your total income on a monthly and annual basis.

The other side of the equation is understanding your expenses, which tend to culminate into a larger figure than many initially anticipate, owing to 'invisible' or 'forgotten' costs. These expenses can be bifurcated into two categories: fixed and variable.

```
[horizontal]
'Fixed expenses':: These are your recurring, predictable
costs such as mortgage or rent payments, car payments,
utility bills, insurance, subscriptions, and minimum
debt payments.
'Variable expenses':: These fluctuate from month to
month, and can often be controlled to some degree. They
include groceries, gas or public transit costs, leisure
```

To understand your expenses, you could monitor and record every dollar spent for a month. Remember to ascertain occasional but inevitable spending, such as car maintenance or medical spending. Alternatively, you can review your debit and credit card statements for the previous few months to get an accurate snapshot of your expenditures.

4.2. Creating a Budget

Once you've gauged your cash inflow and outflow, it's time to form a budget. A typically suggested method, the 50/30/20 approach, suggests splitting your income as:

```
[horizontal]
'50%':: Necessities ▯ allocate approximately half your
post-tax income to needs (fixed expenses, groceries,
basic personal supplies).
'30%':: Wants ▯ Allot 30% to discretionary or non-
essential items (vacations, entertainment).
'20%':: Savings ▯ Put away one-fifth of your income into
savings or towards paying off debts.
```

The idea behind the pro-rata allocation is to incorporate a balance of meeting today's needs, personal enjoyment, and future financial stability.

4.3. Using Budgeting Tools

In the age of digitization, a plethora of free and paid budgeting tools/apps exist to make the process simpler and more dynamic. Apps such as Mint, PocketGuard, and Personal Capital, among others, can sync with various accounts and automatically categorize expenses, track spending, and even provide reminders to ensure you never miss a bill.

However, the magic in these tools lies in their accurate utilization. Make sure to regularly update the application if any of your spending doesn't fall into the correct category.

4.4. Adjusting your Budget over Time

Your budget is not set in stone; it's a dynamic, adaptable tool that must evolve with personal circumstances and economic fluctuations. Major life events, such as marriage, having a child, buying a house, or unexpected job loss, all warrant an immediate review and revamp of your budget.

Setting up periodic reviews, say monthly or quarterly, can also help modify your budget, helping to map necessary changes in spending behavior, or identify potential areas of saving or investment.

4.5. The Power of an Emergency Fund

No amount of budgeting can forecast unpredictable adversities such as a sudden job loss, health emergency, or urgent home or car repairs. Therefore, creating an emergency fund must be an integral part of your budgeting plan. Ideally, it should have enough to cover 3-6 months' worth of living expenses. Start building your fund with regular, small contributions and keep growing it till your targeted cushion amount is hit, and remember, it's only for emergencies.

Budgeting stands as a personal translation of complex economic theory into a tangible, simple approach towards managing finances.

A successful budget sets the foundation for strong financial habits –
undeniably a gateway towards wealth acquisition and financial
independence. While the path may seem intricate at the outset,
embracing the art of budgeting paves the way to take control of your
finances, build wealth, and secure a prosperous future.

Chapter 5. Emergency Funds: Preparation for Unforeseen Events

Emergencies can hit us anytime, often without warning - losing your job, car breaking down, health issues, or natural disasters can abruptly jolt us out of our everyday life's smooth rhythm. These unforeseen occurrences could impose a significant finanical burden, quickly depleting your savings in a blink of an eye. That's where an emergency fund plays a crucial role: it is a financial buffer that protects you against these volatile unpredicted circumstances.

5.1. Why An Emergency Fund is Essential

The notion that an emergency fund is a luxury rather than a necessity is a widely-held but fundamentally misguided idea. The importance of an emergency fund doesn't just lie in the protection it offers during tough financial times. An emergency fund's real value emerges as it aids you in maintaining your standard of living without being forced into debt or sacrificing your long-term financial goals.

1. **Peace of Mind:** The most immediate benefit of an emergency fund is the peace of mind it provides. Knowing you have a safety net to rely on in case of emergencies relieves mental stress, allowing you to focus on resolving the situation rather than worrying about finances.

2. **Protects Your Investments:** An emergency fund can prevent you from resorting to liquidating your investments when an unforeseen incident occurs. By doing so, you're ensuring your investments remain untouched and contributing towards your

longer-term wealth acquisition journey.

3. **Avoids Accumulation of Debt:** With sufficient emergency savings, you can rescue yourself from falling into a debt trap, thereby saving yourself from high-interest repayments that could strain your financial future.

5.2. Building Your Emergency Fund

The key ingredient behind the success of building an emergency fund is consistency. Adhering to a structured saving plan will ensure gradual but stable growth of your emergency funding. Yet, many people question how much they should save, where they should keep their emergency funds, and how to find the extra cash to save monthly.

1. **How Much to Save:** Your emergency fund should ideally cover three to six months' worth of living expenses. However, this amount should be assessed based on personal circumstances such as job security, health conditions, and the number of dependent family members.

2. **Where to Keep the Fund:** Accessibility is a vital factor in deciding where to keep your emergency fund. High-yield savings accounts, money market accounts, or short-term certificates of deposit (CDs) are good choices. These options offer higher interest rates compared to a regular savings account, and you can easily access your funds when an emergency arises.

3. **Where to Find the Money:** Savings might seem difficult, especially if you're living paycheck to paycheck. However, automatically routing a percentage of your income into a dedicated account can make this process much more manageable. Identifying and cutting back on discretionary spending can also free up a considerable amount of money for your emergency fund.

5.3. Overcoming Barriers to Savings

Whilst creating an emergency fund seems straightforward, the reality can pose certain difficulties. There are psychological, practical, and financial barriers that can disrupt the momentum of your savings. Developing a clear understanding of these hurdles and finding solutions can empower you to carve a successful savings path:

1. **Prioritizing Savings:** One of the most common barriers people face while building an emergency fund is the prioritization of immediate wants over future needs. Making savings a priority and considering it a fixed expenditure, similar to rent or utility bills, is a strategic approach to this problem. An 'out of sight, out of mind' attitude can also prevent you from spending your saved funds prematurely.

2. **Setting Realistic Goals:** Setting an unrealistically high savings target can discourage you, especially with sporadic progress. Instead, setting smaller, achievable goals can provide a sense of accomplishment and motivate you to save consistently.

5.4. Review and Revise

Finally, bear in mind that financial planning isn't a static process. It demands regular reviews and revisions. As your income and expenses change over time or due to changes in dependents, commitments, or any drastic life events, so should your emergency fund. Ensuring your emergency fund continues to cover your living expenses for a said period helps you adapt to changes in circumstances, ensuring your financial security.

In conclusion, an emergency fund may not create wealth. However, it preserves your wealth, protects you from slides into debt, and gives you peace of mind. And that, in the grand scheme of financial planning, is priceless. By using the strategies detailed in this chapter, you can effectively build a robust emergency fund that serves as your financial lifeboat, providing stability and security to navigate even through the roughest financial storms.

Chapter 6. The Power of Savings: Small Steps, Big Rewards

In the quest for financial prosperity, the importance of savings cannot be overstated. Not only does it provide a safety net in case of emergencies, but it also acts as a ladder to achieving your financial ambitions. Yet cultivating a habit of saving is often seen as an uphill task. This perception largely stems from the seemingly slow pace at which savings accumulate and the associated self-discipline needed to continually commit a portion of your income to savings. However, with a proper understanding of the fundamentals and benefits associated with saving, you can start to see these small steps yielding big rewards.

6.1. Understanding Savings

To make the best out of savings, it's important first to understand what it entails. Basically, saving is the portion of your income that is not spent but instead set aside for future use. On a deeper level, saving can be seen as delaying present gratification for future benefits. It's a conscious decision to forego current consumption for future financial health and wealth.

For savings to be effective, it must be consistent. But it's not just about setting aside a random amount of money; it requires you to consciously plan and allocate a specific portion of your income towards savings regularly.

6.2. The Importance of Savings

The notion of saving can be likened to the ancient wisdom of sowing seeds. The seeds represent your savings, and the potential harvest stands for the compound growth of your finances. Substantial growth is not achieved overnight but rather takes time, patience, and nurturing.

A key reason for saving is to create an emergency fund. This will act as your financial safety net in case of a sudden, unforeseen event such as job loss, lengthy illness, or a large unexpected expense. The common rule of thumb is to save at least three months' worth of living expenses in your emergency fund.

Savings also present you with the flexibility to seize investment opportunities. An opportunity may come knocking at a time when you least expect it. A well-stocked savings chest makes it easier to take advantage of such opportunities without disrupting your daily cash flow.

Savings accumulate interest over time and this earning potential increases with compound interest. Even small amounts add up over time with the power of compounding.

Savings can also enable you to afford big-ticket items like a house, a car, or education without getting into debt or denting your monthly cash flow.

6.3. Cultivating a Savings Habit

One of the key hurdles to saving is the misconception that it requires large amounts of money. On the contrary, the trick lies in starting small but being consistent.

To develop a saving habit, consider automating your savings. Direct a portion of your paycheck to your savings account even before you start spending. This practice, known as 'paying yourself first,' ensures that you consistently save the chosen amount every month.

Budgeting is another critical aspect of savings. By allocating money to each necessary expense and assigning the remaining funds to savings, you can keep track of your finances better. Be sure to stick to your budget and avoid impulse spending.

Understanding the difference between wants and needs is fundamental. Needs are items that are essential for your daily functioning, while wants are things that you desire but can live without. Prioritizing needs over wants helps to curtail unnecessary expenditure, conducing a better saving rate.

6.4. The Magic of Compound Interest

When it comes to savings, patience truly is a virtue. Due to the magic of compound interest, your savings grow much faster the longer they are left untouched.

To benefit from compound interest, you need to reinvest the interest you earn, instead of spending it. Over time, you'll earn interest on the initial amount you saved, plus the interest you've previously earned. This is what's known as compounding. Over long periods, this can lead to exponential growth of your savings.

Though the progression may seem slow initially, the acceleration of growth over time can be astonishing. This is a practical example of the famous quote, "The greatest reward comes to those who wait."

6.5. Saving vs. Investing

While saving is a critical step towards financial freedom, it's not the end of it. Investment is the next crucial step after saving. Investing involves using your savings to generate more income or capital gains. When done right, it can significantly expedite your journey to wealth acquisition.

However, investing comes with its risk. Hence, having a solid saving base before venturing into investing can cushion you from potential loss. Moreover, it's recommended to gain some basic financial literacy and understanding of investment options before committing your money.

6.6. Final Thoughts

Embracing the power of savings to effect significant financial growth demands determination, discipline, and patience. It might feel arduous at first, but you'll be surprised by the impact of small, consistent saving steps over the longer term. Remember, the journey to financial freedom isn't raced overnight. It's steadily won by making careful, consistent, and informed financial decisions, one of the most important being savings.

By harnessing the power of savings, adhering to the principles laid out in this chapter, you'll be well on your path towards securing a bright financial future. The key is to start now, no matter how small, and consistently build a robust savings base that will act as the launchpad to your wealth acquisition journey.

Chapter 7. Debt Management: Strategies for Freedom

Before we delve into the world of debt management strategies, it's crucial to understand the concept of debt in its entirety. Debt, often seen with a negative connotation, is an integral component of our financial lives. From student loans to credit cards, mortgages to car loans, we are all likely to encounter debt at some point in our journey. However, when managed correctly, debt can be a powerful instrument, directing us towards a progressive financial future.

7.1. Understanding Debt

We begin by comprehending the nature of debt. Firstly, it's important to differentiate between 'good' and 'bad' debt. Good debt, such as mortgages or student loans, are investments that, in the long run, can increase your wealth. Bad debts, conversely, depreciate in value over time. Your brand-new designer clothes, that flashy car, or the high-interest credit cards are all examples of bad debt that are best avoided, if possible. Recognizing the nature of your debt is the first step towards effective management.

7.2. Debt Repayment Methods

Now, let's drill down into the approaches one can adopt to repay debts.

1. The Avalanche Method: In this arrangement, one organizes their debts from the highest to lowest interest rate. The emphasis is on paying more towards the highest-interest debt while making minimum payments on the rest. Once the highest-interest debt is settled, you move to the next on the list, and this continues in an 'avalanche.' This method, though requiring more patience, likely

saves most on interest.

2. The Snowball Method: In contrast, this strategy requires organizing debt from smallest to largest balances, disregarding the interest rates. One pays more toward the smallest debt and the minimum on the others until the smallest is paid off. Then, you roll over what you were paying on the now settled debt to the next smallest debt, continuing until all debts are cleared. This method provides quick wins, promoting motivation and momentum.

It is essential to choose a repayment strategy that aligns with your behavioral tendencies and financial goals.

7.3. Creating a Budget

With the understanding of debt types and repayment mechanisms, the next step to freedom from debt is formulating a budget. A good budget reflects your financial goals and prioritizes necessary expenditures. It should account for every income source and allocate those resources towards necessary expenditure, discretionary spending, savings, and of course, debt repayment.

7.4. Negotiating With Creditors

Believe it or not, sometimes it is possible to negotiate the terms of your debts. You may be able to reduce the interest rate, change your payment schedule, or even reduce your debt by negotiating with your creditors.

7.5. Living below Your Means

As old-school as it may sound, living below your means is often the most potent weapon in your arsenal against debt. The idea is to trim unnecessary expenditures and to redirect those savings towards debt repayment and wealth creation.

7.6. Developing Additional Income Streams

While cutting back on spending is effective, generating additional income can expedite your journey to a debt-free life. Such income streams can come from a variety of sources: a second job, freelance work, or a small-scale business, to name a few.

7.7. Adopting a Healthy Financial Lifestyle

Eliminating debt does not guarantee freedom from it in perpetuity. Maintaining a healthy financial lifestyle is crucial. This includes a regular review of finances, continuous learning about financial management, wise use of credit, and of course, saving and investing strategically.

In this chapter, we've aimed to demystify debt and demonstrate the effectiveness of certain management strategies in combating it. Embrace these principles, apply them diligently, and watch as your financial health transforms, allowing you the freedom to seize the opportunities life has to offer.

Chapter 8. Investment Essentials: From Novice to Knowledgeable

Decoding the jargon that surrounds the realm of investments is the first step on your journey from novice to knowledgeable. In this chapter, we will peel back the layers of complexity, simplifying things for you so you can confidently make informed investment decisions.

8.1. Understanding Basics

First things first – one must understand the basics of investment. An investment refers to the allocation of money in something with the expectation of generating an income or profit. There are several types of investments to choose from, such as stocks, bonds, real estate, mutual funds, and more. Each of these options has its own set of advantages and disadvantages, and it's crucial to grasp these before you begin investing.

8.2. Risk and Return

In the world of investments, "risk" and "return" are two commonly used terms. Risk refers to the possibility that you might lose some or all of your original investment. Return, on the other hand, is the money you earn on your investments. The fundamental principle of investing is that risk and return are directly proportional. Higher the risk, greater is the potential return, and vice versa.

8.3. Diversifying Investments

Investing all your money in one place isn't advisable. Diversification, or spreading your investments across different types of assets, can help reduce risk while still providing a good return on investment. Stocks, bonds, and cash are the main asset classes you can diversify your investments across. How you divide your investments between these various asset classes is termed asset allocation.

8.4. Stocks: The Game Changer

Now, let's dive deeper into the most popular investment instrument: stocks. When you own a company's stock, you own a piece of that company. Stocks are a great way to grow your wealth, but they come with their own set of challenges. Understanding these challenges and learning how to deal with them can be the key to successful investing.

8.5. Bonds: The Safe Harbour

Bonds represent loans made by investors to entities (like government or companies) which pay a fixed interest over a specified period, and then return the original amount at the end of that period. Bonds are seen as 'safe' investments because the risk of default is generally low, and returns are predictable.

8.6. Real Estate: The Tangible Asset

Investing in real estate can be a profitable venture if done right – thanks to the predictable cash flow, excellent returns, tax advantages, and diversification. Renting, selling, and even merely holding properties to appreciate in value can make real estate a worthwhile investment.

8.7. Mutual Funds: Diverse and Accessible

A mutual fund is a pool of funds collected from multiple investors to invest in securities like stocks, bonds, money market instruments, and more. Mutual funds allow individuals to participate in diversified portfolios, which offer a degree of safety due to their diversified nature.

8.8. Portfolio Management

Once you have investments in various classes, managing them effectively becomes paramount. Portfolio management involves making informed decisions about investment mix and policy, asset allocation for individuals and institutions, and balancing risk against performance.

8.9. Staying Current

Investing isn't a one-time action. It requires constant monitoring, adjustments and staying updated on market trends and macroeconomic changes. This continual adjustment is necessary to optimise returns and manage risk effectively.

In summary, investment is a journey, not a destination. It requires diligence, knowledge and constant review and analysis. Equip yourself with understanding and continually enhance it. Embrace the dynamic nature of markets and learn from each investment decision. Remember, every investor starts as a novice, and becoming knowledgeable is a process – a process that begins with understanding the essentials. This chapter was your starting point; the journey ahead will be transformative.

Chapter 9. Insurance and Risk Management: Safeguarding Your Assets

The modern world is laden with risk and uncertainty; consider financial risk as the Joker in the deck, its inclusion in the game changes strategies entirely. So let's explore the stage where insurance and risk management stand, scenarios where they take the spotlight, and the strategies that will cast these supporting actors in our financial design.

9.1. Role of Insurance in Financial Planning

Insurance doesn't just financially protect us against potential losses; it's the invisible buffer safeguarding us from economic fallout, a silent ally in risk management. One might question its necessity, but bear in mind, it's not the prevalence but the potential magnitude of risk that deems insurance vital. Alan Lakein famously said, "Planning is bringing the future into the present so that you can do something about it now." As you set the stage for wealth acquisition, remember that any goal without a plan is just a wish. With this in mind, integrating insurance into your financial blueprint is as necessary as building solid walls around your dream castle.

9.2. Understanding Risk Management

Risk management entails identifying, analyzing, assessing, and seeking methods to mitigate potential financial losses. Like a detective working through clues to solve a mystery, effective risk management helps identify significant threats and design solutions to counter them. Contrary to common belief, it's not exclusive to businesses or large-scale operations; it's a crucial instrument, humming quietly in the backbone of personal financial planning.

1. Risk Assessment: Your first step is conducting a comprehensive risk assessment. It's your personal reconnaissance expedition, scanning the terrains of your life for potential pitfalls that could hinder your financial progress. There are "what ifs" that could derail or delay your wealth acquisition journey - long term illness, property damage, litigation, death, unemployment, etc. A thorough risk assessment elucidates these scenarios and sets the foundation for the subsequent stage.

2. Risk Management Strategies: Upon identifying potential risks, adopt strategies to manage them. Financial buffs might be quick to propose 'risk sharing' or 'risk transfer,' and they'd be right! It's here where insurance raises its hand and offers itself as the perfect solution – a quintessential risk transfer mechanism.

9.3. Insurance as a Risk Transfer Mechanism

Insurance, in the simplest terms, is a legal agreement that promises compensation for certain losses in exchange for regular payments, known as premiums. It's like paying someone else to handle the aftermath of a potential disaster. It doesn't lessen the occurrence of the risk but lessens its financial impact, fortifying you against drastic financial shifts.

1. Life and Health Insurance: Navigating the sea of life and health insurance policies can seem daunting. But stripped down to the basics, they compensate for the financial impact of any health issues or death. Temporary incapacity or long-term illness could disrupt income streams. Similarly, an unfortunate event leading

to death would inflict financial stress on dependents. These insurance policies are the lifeboats on your financial cruise ship, ensuring you and your family don't drown in a sea of financial instability.

2. Property and Liability Insurance: This category includes home insurance, auto insurance, and other insurance types covering tangible assets. Property insurance safeguards against financial loss arising from damage to assets like houses, cars, etc. Liability insurance, on the other hand, protects against potential lawsuits or claims due to negligence, malpractice, or accidents.

3. Long-Term Disability Insurance: This insurance kicks in when a significant health issue prevents you from working for an extended period. It provides a sizable percentage of your income during the disability, securing your financial stability.

4. Long-Term Care Insurance: Long-term care insurance is a safety net for potential extensive care expenses due to chronic medical conditions, disability, or disorder. As one ages, the chance of requiring long-term care increases, which could have severe financial implications without appropriate insurance in place.

While some might argue that premiums paid towards insurance could instead be invested for higher returns, remember our friend Mr. Risk from earlier. It disrupts your well-laid plans, replacing steady calm with tempestuous uncertainty. Insurance, then, is the anchor preventing your financial ship from being tossed around in this chaotic storm.

9.4. Conclusion

To wrap up, insurance and risk management aren't mere extras in your financial blueprint; they're part and parcel of its solid structure. Building wealth without securing it is akin to building castles on unstable sand. So, integrate insurance into your financial planning, understand its myriad faces, and most importantly, remember – the best time to consider insurance and risk management isn't after a calamity; it's right now. Knowing the risks and managing them effectively ensures that no matter the financial storms, your wealth acquisition journey remains steady, and your financial future, secure.

Chapter 10. Retirement Planning: Securing Your Golden Years

Understanding the importance of planning for your retirement is the first step to securing your golden years. In this chapter, we will walk you through a comprehensive roadmap of retirement planning, distilling it into tangible steps and considerations, so you are equipped with the necessary knowledge to make smart decisions about your future.

10.1. The Importance of Retirement Planning

Retirement planning is paramount to achieving financial satisfaction later in life. You may wish to travel, take up new hobbies, or simply enjoy a comfortable lifestyle without the need to work. However, without a well-sketched retirement plan, these dreams may stay just that - dreams. Proper planning allows you to:

1. Determine your retirement income goals

2. Make informed decisions to accomplish these goals

3. Review regularly to adapt to changes

10.2. Assess Your Retirement Needs

We all have diverse aspirations for our retirement, and thus our financial needs will vary. Evaluate your retirement goals to estimate the amount of savings you need.

1. Calculate your annual expenses post-retirement, accounting for

inflation.

2. Consider any potential major expenses, such as healthcare or travel.

3. Determine potential income sources like Social Security, pension, or part-time jobs.

10.3. Retirement Savings and Investment Options

There are several methods of saving for retirement; choosing the right ones can make a substantial difference in your financial stability.

10.3.1. 401(k)

A 401(k) or similar employer-sponsored retirement plan is a godsend for those seeking to accumulate a sizable retirement portfolio. In this tax-advantaged plan, your contributions are made pre-tax, reducing your taxable income now. Some employers match a portion of your contributions, effectively giving you free money.

10.3.2. Individual Retirement Accounts

There are two primary types of IRAs - Traditional and Roth.

Traditional IRA: Contributions may be tax-deductible, but you'll owe taxes when you withdraw the funds.

Roth IRA: Contributions aren't tax-deductible, but withdrawals in retirement are tax-free.

10.3.3. Annuities

An annuity is a contract between you and an insurance company. You make an investment in the annuity, and it then makes payments to you on a future date or series of dates. These returns can be variable or fixed.

10.4. Early Withdrawal Penalties

While saving for retirement, it's crucial to understand that retirement funds are designed primarily for retirement, and early withdrawals can come with heavy penalties. Know the implications before you tap into these funds prematurely.

10.5. Estate Planning

Estate planning is an often overlooked, but crucial aspect of retirement planning. Arguably as important as the planning of your savings, estate planning ensures your assets are appropriately distributed per your wishes upon your passing.

10.5.1. Wills

A legal document, a will primarily provides instructions for distributing your assets after your death.

10.5.2. Trusts

A trust is a fiduciary arrangement that allows a third party, or trustee, to hold assets on behalf of a beneficiary.

10.6. Frequent Review and Adjustment

An effective retirement plan isn't a set-it-and-forget-it plan. It must be constantly reviewed, and tweaks must be made as necessary.

Regularly revisit your retirement plan to ensure it still aligns with your current situation and goals.

Retirement planning may seem a daunting task, but by breaking it down step-by-step and examining each element thoroughly, it becomes more digestible. The time, effort, and thought you invest now will pay off later in life, allowing you to enjoy your golden years to the fullest.

Chapter 11. Estate Planning: Wealth Transmission and Legacy Creation

Estate planning is not often perceived as an exciting topic, but when comprehensively understood and effectively executed, it has the power to define a lasting legacy while assuring that your accumulated wealth is transmitted in accordance to your desires.

11.1. Understanding Estate Planning

Let's start by defining estate planning. It involves making arrangements for the dispersal of your assets upon death, eliminating uncertainties over administration, and maximizing the estate's value by reducing taxes and other associated expenses. It includes bequests (gifts left in a will), assignment of power of attorney, beneficiaries on life insurance policies, pension plans, or a trust fund.

Estate planning is an ongoing process and should be started as soon as one has any measurable asset base. An effective estate plan helps individuals put financial affairs in order, ensure the best care for dependents, and align their wealth with their goals and values.

11.2. The Importance of an Estate Plan

Whether you're a millionaire or a middle-class breadwinner, everyone should have an estate plan. Here's why:

- A well-crafted estate plan ensures that your hard-earned assets are distributed according to your wishes after you're gone.

- It can protect your spouse, children, or other heirs from heavy taxes and legal complications.

- If you are incapacitated, it can save your family from making tough decisions at a difficult time.

11.3. Components of an Estate Plan

At the core of a successful estate plan are a few key documents. These can include:

- Will: The cornerstone of an estate plan, a will direct your assets, nominates an executor, assigns guardians for your children, and spells out how to distribute your assets upon your death.

- Durable Power of Attorney (POA): This document nominates a party to act on your behalf if you're incapacitated.

- Healthcare Proxy: Also known as a healthcare POA, this document nominates a party to make medical decisions on your behalf if you can't.

- Living Will: This contains your directives on end-of-life decisions.

These documents form the basic building blocks of your estate plan.

11.4. Implementing an Effective Estate Plan

Creating an effective estate plan is a multi-step process involving collaboration with professionals.

- *Evaluate your assets*: Itemize all of your assets, including properties, investments, retirement savings, insurance policies, and business interests.

- *Identify your objectives*: Understand what you want your wealth to accomplish. This could be retirement income, tuition for grandchildren, charitable contributions, etc.

- *Formulate a strategy*: With objectives in place, tailor your estate plan to these goals. Engage professionals to assist with the legal and tax aspects.

- *Implement your plan*: Work with an attorney to create the necessary legal documents. Regularly review and update them according to changes in assets or personal circumstances.

- *Monitor it*: Like your investment portfolio, an estate plan should be reviewed and adjusted as needed.

11.5. Particular Strategies for Wealth Transmission

1. *Gifting*: While alive, one can give away wealth up to certain limits without incurring taxes. It's crucial to work with a tax professional to stay within legal bounds.

2. *Trusts*: Trusts come in several varieties and can serve different purposes according to your financial goals and circumstances.

3. *Life insurance*: Policies can provide liquidity for estate taxes, protect an asset's value, or even serve as inheritance.

11.6. Legacy Creation

Creating a legacy isn't just about passing wealth - it's about passing values. Charitable giving, establishing scholarships, and creating family foundations are just some of the ways you can impart meaningful legacies. It's essential to work closely with professionals to ensure that your desired legacy is viable, legal, and meets tax requirements.

To conclude, estate planning is an essential aspect of financial planning. It isn't something that should be postponed until old age or wealth accumulation. An effective estate plan can offer peace of mind, knowing your hard-earned wealth will positively impact the lives of your loved ones or support the causes you believe in. Estate planning is where life's work meets legacy, and by actively engaging today, you can ensure your legacy flourishes tomorrow.

(Note: Asciidoc syntax used for formatting purposes and might not render properly in certain text editors viewing raw text.)

www.ingramcontent.com/pod-product-compliance
Lightning Source LLC
Chambersburg PA
CBHW071042260726
48661CB00007B/3116